A Sanctuary in our Midst

ENDORSEMENTS

"Karen Straszheim's *A Sanctuary in Our Midst* will help you prepare for the Christmas season. She presents the Scriptures in a way that both refreshes the believer in Jesus and answers many questions of those who are seeking the true meaning of Christmas. Karen helps the reader understand the importance of preparing the heart for Christmas. It is refreshing in application and focuses upon God's Word. Most of all, *A Sanctuary in Our Midst* will help you see, "Believing in Jesus is different than being religious.""

-PASTOR EARL KORHONEN

World Missions Director, Association of Free Lutheran Congregations

"When I was young I fondly remember the church we attended did something that made quite an impression on me. Each year, after Christmas they removed the lights, decorations and all the branches from the beautiful large tree that stood in the front. At Easter time the trunk from that same Christmas tree became the symbol for the Cross of Christ's Crucifixion. When Christmas came each year I began to anticipate this transformation - looking not just at the outward beauty but past the branches to the very center of the tree. The author has done the same thing in this devotional. The daily readings and questions point to the incredible connection between Christmas and Easter making the Gospel of Christ the very heart of it all. It is a wonderful way to anticipate the holidays. 'Thanks be to God for His indescribable gift!' (2 Cor. 9:15)."

-JENNIFER VOSS-WHITE

Student of the Word, Servant of Christ, Women's Ministry Leader

"Looking for ways to better prepare your heart for the coming of Christ? This devotional is full of inspiration. Karen does an excellent job of using Scripture to lead the reader through prophesies and their fulfillment. Everyday testimonies help to apply these truths to our lives today."

-Jan McDermott

Retired Bible Camp Director, Riverside Lutheran Bible Camp, Story City, Iowa

"Karen Straszheim's use of Scripture is appropriate and consistent with the character of the Christ follower that I know her to be. Karen has a deep respect for the authority of the Bible and I have seen her apply it when serving on our short-mission projects here in Czech Republic. Also, her use of Scripture is an essential point in the Gospel: Jesus' nativity is the fulfillment of our prophesied Messiah. Karen leads the student to a deep understanding of the Advent message and restores the real message of Christmas. I wish the reader could see her in action when leading non-believers to the centrality of the Scripture, the preeminence of Jesus as our sin bearer, and hear the loving care in her voice. Karen is a true and competent evangelist . . . intelligent, gentle, and forthright. I hope you will experience her evangelical gift here in her devotional."

-Curt Mobley

Teacher of English at the Evangelical Theological Seminary of Prague, Czech Republic, and Missionary with ReachGlobal

Illustrations by Matthew Reierson

A Sanctuary in Our Midst

Christmas Reflections on Jesus

Karen L. Straszheim

Ambassador International
GREENVILLE, SOUTH CAROLINA & BELFAST, NORTHERN IRELAND
www.ambassador-international.com

A Sanctuary in Our Midst

©2019 by Karen L. Straszheim
All rights reserved

ISBN: 978-1-62020-720-8
eISBN: 978-1-62020-739-0

Illustrations by Matthew Reierson

No part of this publication may be reproduced, distributed, or transmitted in any form or by any means, including photocopying, recording, or other electronic or mechanical methods, without the prior written permission of the publisher, except in the case of brief quotations embodied in critical reviews and certain other noncommercial uses permitted by copyright law. For permission requests, contact the publisher using the information below.

Scripture quotations are taken from The Holy Bible, New International Version, NIV Copyright 1984 by Biblica, Inc. Used by permission. All rights reserved worldwide.

and

The Message, Copyright 2002. Used by permission of NavPress Publishing Group.

Cover Design and Page Layout by Hannah Nichols
eBook Conversion by Anna Riebe Raats

AMBASSADOR INTERNATIONAL
Emerald House
411 University Ridge, Suite B14
Greenville, SC 29601, USA
www.ambassador-international.com

AMBASSADOR BOOKS
The Mount
2 Woodstock Link
Belfast, BT6 8DD, Northern Ireland, UK
www.ambassadormedia.co.uk

The colophon is a trademark of Ambassador, a Christian publishing company.

To the King of glory and the current and coming generations of those who seek Him (Ps. 24:6-7).

TABLE OF CONTENTS

CHAPTER ONE
INTRODUCTION   13

This book is about what it is to know Jesus. It was written to help you come closer to Him whose coming we celebrate at Christmas.

CHAPTER TWO
GOOD TIDINGS: JESUS HAS COME   21

The tidings of Christmas are good because all are blessed through Jesus.

CHAPTER THREE
A LOVED CHILD   27

You aren't unloved or abandoned in the Christmas season. He will listen and be there for you.

CHAPTER FOUR
THE CREATOR OF LIFE   31

The birth of Jesus was planned and brought about by the Creator. He has a plan for you, too.

CHAPTER FIVE
GREAT JOY FOR ALL PEOPLE   37

If we could be good enough for God by following rules, there would be no need for Jesus, a Savior or Christmas. But all people have a need for Him.

CHAPTER SIX
A SPIRIT OF GRACE AND SUPPLICATION   43

When we come to Him humbly asking for forgiveness, He reassures us of a restored relationship with Himself.

CHAPTER SEVEN
SELF-SEEKING OR GOD-SEEKING?   49

Those with their heart or mind set on things will have a different kind of Christmas than those who are set on Him.

CHAPTER EIGHT
THE FOUNDATION STONE   53

Jesus is a dear, beloved Rock of inestimable value. He is a unique gift.

CHAPTER NINE
JESUS THE COMPASSIONATE KING   59

Jesus is known for His mercy, different from many other rulers.

CHAPTER TEN
WHO DO YOU SAY I AM?   65

Jesus is more than a man or a baby in a story, and belief in Him is more than being religious.

CHAPTER ELEVEN
DOING THE UNEXPECTED   71

When God proclaims a holiday, He knows how to help us celebrate.

ENDNOTES   75

ABOUT THE ARTWORK BY MATTHEW REIERSON   77

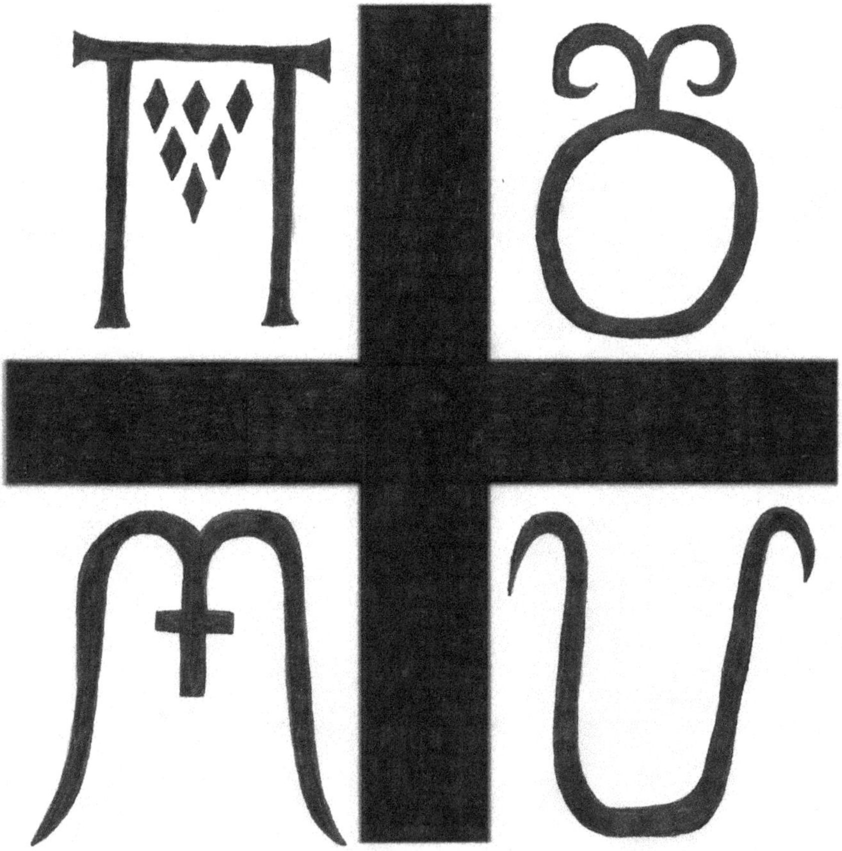

1.

INTRODUCTION

"In view of his appearing and his kingdom, I give you this charge: Preach the Word; be prepared in season and out of season: correct, rebuke and encourage - with great patience and careful instruction" (2 Tim. 4:1-2, NIV).[1]

THE INSPIRATION TO WRITE ABOUT Jesus has come from different places. The first is from my reading and studying of the Word. I learned early in my Christian life that the New Testament and Old Testament both help the understanding of the other. A passage in the New Testament often corresponds to a passage in the Old Testament and a person gets a better understanding of a subject when the passages are read together. The Scofield Bible says, "The Bible is its own best interpreter. Its message in one place is almost always illuminated by texts elsewhere in Scripture . . . The Bible sheds its own light."[2]

Jesus helped us know how to read Scripture in this way. For example, early in His teaching in His hometown of Nazareth, He stood up to read in the synagogue.

" . . . The scroll of the prophet Isaiah was handed to him. Unrolling it, he found the place . . . " where it wrote about Him. 'The Spirit of the Lord is on me, because he has anointed me to preach good news to the poor. He has sent me to proclaim freedom for the prisoners and recovery of sight for the blind, to release the oppressed, to proclaim the year of the Lord's favor' . . . The eyes of everyone in the synagogue were fastened on him and He began by saying to them, 'Today this scripture is fulfilled in your hearing'" (Luke 4:17-21).

He taught people to understand Him by reading them a prophecy from Isaiah 61:1-2 in the Old Testament, written 600-700 years before He lived. Today, we have both Isaiah in the Old Testament and the account of Luke in the New Testament, with a greater understanding of Jesus coming from reading both passages.

The second inspiration to write came from what I learned about Jesus from my late husband, Keith Reierson. Keith was a pastor whose heart was to teach the Word and help people understand who God is from Scripture. I was in his Sunday school classes, asked him questions, and lived with him at home for eighteen years. Our family lost the privilege of his presence when he was killed in a car accident in 2004. While he was here, I learned from him the surprising number of ways Jesus fulfilled prophecies in the Old Testament. Keith wrote a devotional booklet for families with twenty-four prophecies to be read in preparation for Christmas. Unfortunately, the location of the book isn't known, but the inspiration of it is remembered. That devotional was a great instrument for my understanding of who Jesus is.

Others have also written about prophecies fulfilled by Jesus. Some Bibles have a list or chart showing Old Testament prophecies and New Testament fulfillment. The *Complete Jewish Bible* is good place to look for such a chart.[3] A summary of the main prophecies found in this Bible is located at the end of the chapter. A Jewish New Testament, *The New Covenant Prophecy Edition*, shows references to the Old Testament in bold type throughout the chapters in the book. A person looking through it can see the large number of passages from the Old that are found again the New.

The main focus of writing about prophecies fulfilled in Jesus is that Jesus is the promised Messiah. People in the Bible were waiting for generations for the Anointed One to arrive. Isaiah 53 is an entire Old Testament chapter that describes the one who "poured out his life unto death, and was numbered with the transgressors. For he bore the sin of many, and made intercession for the transgressors" (Isaiah 53:12). In the New Testament in Luke 3:15, it says that "the people were waiting expectantly and were all wondering in their hearts if John might possibly be the Messiah." The woman in John 4 was anticipating him. She said, "Come, see a man who told me everything I ever did. Could this be the Christ" (John 4:29)?[4]

Others write to convince others of a related idea, that Jesus is the Son of God, for example, Josh McDowell in *More Than A Carpenter.* This author writes about coincidence and statistical probability. The goal of the writing is to show that the chance of one person, specifically Jesus, fulfilling all of what was written about Him in the Bible is infinitesimally small. It isn't just a coincidence that Jesus seems to be the promised Messiah. It is something we can have confidence in because of the large number of prophecies that came true.

When thinking about writing this book, I did not see a need to redo what has been written in other places. I asked to Lord to think with me about how to write about Jesus, the prophecies, and Christmas. What is on these pages has been collected from my quiet times with Him. When I am with Jesus and read the Word, I often leave feeling there is something He has given me that I would love others to know about, too. What is here is offered in the spirit of those in Acts 4:20 who couldn't help but speak about what they had seen and heard.

A Sanctuary in Our Midst is written for the Christmas season. It can be read as a devotional book or in a group study. There are questions at the end of each chapter to discuss if you are in a group. Different from devotionals that have daily readings for Advent, this book has eleven chapters that can be used as interludes. An interlude is a time that uplifts and invigorates like stepping outside to enjoy a clear December night. The chapters are written to help you leave the bustling of the holiday for a while and find encouragement, vision, and perspective. When there is a later time for quietness, you can read another chapter and let your thinking be further refreshed. Whether read individually or together, I hope that the chapters will help you come closer to Him whose coming we celebrate.

A SANCTUARY IN OUR MIDST
PROPHECIES ABOUT JESUS THE MESSIAH

Prophecy	**Old Testament**	**Fulfilled in New**
Be a descendant of David and heir to his throne	2 Sam. 7:12-13; Isa. 9:7; Jer. 23:5	Matt. 1:1, 6; Acts 13:22-23; Rom. 1:3
Be born of a virgin	Isa. 7:14	Matt. 1:18-23; Luke 1:26-35
Be born in Bethlehem	Mic. 5:2	Matt. 2:1; Luke 2:4-7
Be preceded by one who announced Him	Isa. 40:3; Mal. 3:1	Matt. 3:3; John 3:28
Have a ministry of good news	Isa. 61:1-2	Luke 4:18-19
Enter Jerusalem on a donkey	Zech. 9:9	Mark 11:1-11
Be executed by crucifixion	Ps. 22:1, 16-1; Zech. 12:10	Matt. 27:35-46; Luke 24:39; John 19:18, 34-37; 20:20-28; Rev. 1:7
Be executed without having a bone broken	Exod. 12:46; Ps. 34:21	John 19:31-37
Be the one whose death atones for sins	Isa. 53:5-6,12	Mark 10:45; John 1:29; 3:16

Prophecy	**Old Testament**	**Fulfilled in New**
Be raised from the dead	Isa. 53:10-12; Ps. 16:10	Matt. 28:1-20; Acts 2:23-36; 13:32-37; 1 Cor. 15:3-6
Ascend to heaven	Ps. 16:11; 68:18; 110:1	Luke 24:51; Acts 1:9-11, 7:55; Heb. 1:3
Be the king	Ps. 2:6	John 18:33, 37

GROUP QUESTIONS: CHAPTER ONE

1. What do you think of the statement, "The Bible is its own best interpreter. Its message in one place is almost always illuminated by texts elsewhere in the Scripture?"

2. How do you usually study the Bible? What helps you understand it? What other sources do you use for commentary or interpretation of difficult passages?

3. The Old Testament is especially wearisome and challenging to some. What have you found that helps it be more interesting or relatable to your life?

4. Looking at the chart about prophecies in the Old Testament fulfilled in the New, which ones are new to you? Which ones would you like to learn more about?

5. What does knowing these prophecies were fulfilled do for your confidence in Scripture? How does it influence or affect your ideas about Jesus?

6. What do you hope for this Christmas with family, friends or God? What would you like to be different from other years?

2.

Good Tidings: Jesus Has Come

> "Bring in your idols to tell us what is going to happen. Tell us what the former things were, so that we may consider them and know their final outcome. Or declare to us the things to come, tell us what the future hold so that we may know you are gods . . . See, the former things have taken place and new things I declare; before they spring into being I announce them to you" (Isa. 41:22-23; 42:9).

THE PASSAGE ABOVE FROM ISAIAH 41 and 42 describes the way most of us think of prophecy: "before [things] spring into being I announce them to you." The "I" in this sentence is God. We can learn what God has planned since He gave knowledge to a prophet to write it down for us. The New Testament helps us understand this also: " . . . no prophecy of Scripture came about by the prophet's own interpretation. For prophecy never had its origin in the will of man but men spoke from God as they were carried along by the Holy Spirit" (2 Pet. 1:20-21).

Isaiah 41:22-23; 42:9 can be read as a question. The passage asks how does a person get the knowledge of a prophet? Who can tell us what has happened before, declare what is going to happen in the future, and know the outcome of all events? This kind of knowledge, where all of what is foretold comes true, is an ability God attributes only to Himself. Do you know anyone else with a mastery of all people and all events in all time? Scripture says if you have this skill, you too might be a god. But in saying this, the writer of Isaiah knows you don't have that knowledge or power and there aren't other gods.

Other gods are what people have made up. "They are all false!" it continues in Isaiah 41:29, "Their deeds amount to nothing; their images are but wind and confusion."

Prophecy from Scripture that has come true is testimony and confirmation that there is one true God who exists. He is the genius who planned and began history. What He has planned is revealed to us in the Bible. People lived and did what was foretold, predicted moments and occasions came about.

For example, it was prophesied in Isaiah 40 that John the Baptist would come before Jesus. The book of Mark in the New Testament begins with this: "I will send my messenger ahead of you, who will prepare your way - a voice of one calling in the desert, prepare the way for the Lord, make straight paths for him." The next sentence is one to contemplate: "And so John came" (Mark 1:2-4). This is how we are to think of prophecy. The man and his message were foretold and so it came to be.

John's assignment was to make ready a people prepared for the Lord: "This was [John's] message: 'After me will come one more powerful than I . . . I baptize you with water, but he will baptize you with the Holy Spirit'" (Mark 1:7-8). John taught that "salvation through the forgiveness of sins" was coming (Luke 1:77). He came before Jesus and later was also a witness of Jesus. He testified about what he knew and saw, that Jesus was the Son of God.

John brought people the gospel, or good news (Luke 3:18). At Christmas, we refer to the gospel as good tidings. The language of good tidings is in Isaiah 40:9, "You who bring good tidings to Zion, go up on a high mountain." and Isaiah 41:27, "I gave to Jerusalem a messenger of good tidings." A question to consider is, what is good about the tidings?

If you go in a store in the weeks before Christmas, you will see a number of things that are advertised as what is good about Christmas. There are lights, decorations, wrapping paper, and ribbons that make our homes lovely. There are also a large variety of gifts to give and receive. For some, what is good about Christmas are the songs people sing or the story of a special baby born on a starlit night.

The Bible gives us one main idea about why the tidings of Christmas are good. Psalm 72:17 says, "All nations will be blessed through him and they will call him blessed." This passage is about Jesus. Isaiah 35 beautifully describes what it will be like when Jesus has come:

> "The desert and parched land will be glad; the wilderness will rejoice and blossom. Like the crocus, it will burst into bloom; it will rejoice greatly and shout for joy . . . They will see the glory of the LORD, the splendor of our God . . . And a highway will be there; it will be called the Way of Holiness . . . But only the redeemed will walk there . . . They will enter Zion with singing; everlasting joy will crown their heads. Gladness and joy will overtake them, and sorrow and sighing will flee away" (Isa. 35:1-2, 8-10).

It will be like this because Jesus saves the needy from death. The redeemed, those who are forgiven through Jesus, will be with Him in heaven (Zion in Isa. 35:9-10 above). Jesus the Savior that we hear about at Christmas came so that we could be where there is greater glory and splendor than what we experience here on earth in the Christmas season.

John and Jesus both taught there was something for a person to do to see this glory and splendor in heaven, repent (Matt. 3:2; 4:17). The person who repents of their sin is the person who is forgiven and saved from death. They are the person who will enter heaven with singing, gladness, and joy (Is. 35:10).

Prophecy in the Old Testament was accompanied by harps, lyres, and cymbals, and thanks and praise to God (1 Chron. 25:1, 3). People in the Bible were glad for what they learned about God from prophecy. At Christmas we also can be glad for what we learn about God from Scripture. One day we will enter heaven with everlasting joy. For now, we can enter Christmas with singing, gladness and joy. He came so we can know Him.

GROUP QUESTIONS: CHAPTER TWO

1. What are some ways people try to know what the future is?

2. Reread this question: "Do you know anyone else with a mastery of all people and all events in all time?" Do you think this is true of God? Do you know of anyone else who claims to do this? What do you think of the claim?

3. For you, what is good about Christmas? What isn't good? What helps sorrow and sighing flee away if that's what you're experiencing in the Christmas season?

4. In the Bible, God's glory is seen in the temple (the church or heaven) and in the sky (read Ezekiel 10:4, 43:4-5; Psalm 19:1). The star of Bethlehem was one example of His glory seen in the heavens. What do you think glory is? If you could see God's glory like the shepherds in Luke 2:9, what would you see?

5. How do you think the glory and splendor of Christmas compares to heaven? What do you look forward to when you go to be with Him?

3.

A Loved Child

"When Israel was a child, I loved him and out of Egypt I called my son" (Hosea 11:1).

WHEN JESUS WAS BORN, THE people in Israel were governed by a Roman king, Herod the Great. Matthew 2 says that when King Herod heard from the Magi (the wise men) that a Jewish king was born, he was disturbed about the challenge to his reign and began to search for the child Jesus to kill him.

An angel appeared to Joseph, Jesus' earthly father, in a dream to tell him about Herod's plan. The angel advised Joseph to flee, so Joseph got up, took the child and his mother during the night and left for Egypt, where they stayed until the death of Herod. Later they returned to Israel and went to live in the town of Nazareth. What the Lord had said through the prophet Hosea was fulfilled: "Out of Egypt I called my son" (Hosea 11:1; Matt. 2:13-14).

In the Old Testament, there was another time when God's people went to Egypt. It was a time of famine. The Israelites went to Egypt to find food and later left the country. In this earlier account, the Lord used the prophet Moses to bring Israel out of Egypt. It was a foreshadowing of Jesus coming out of Egypt as a child and also of His bringing us out of Egypt, from slavery to sin, in the New Testament.

We read in both stories of escape to Egypt that this was how God cared for His people. God is our helper who loves us (Hosea 14:4). His love protects us (John 17:11).

If God had not loved and protected Joseph, Mary, and Jesus, what would have been the outcome for them? In Matthew, it says that "Herod gave orders to kill all the boys in Bethlehem and its vicinity who were two years old and under." There was heard among the people "weeping and great mourning . . . Parents weeping for their children . . . because they [were] no more" (Matt. 2:16,18). But Joseph and Mary returned to Israel with their child still living. God's love was shown to them through the protection of their child's life.

Some people feel unloved or abandoned throughout the year and these feelings are noticed even more in the Christmas season. Our culture says this is a time to be with family. But for some, the people they'd like to be with are absent. A parent hasn't been there for them as a child or an adult. For others, an important person has left, quit, walked out or died, leaving them feeling deserted, cast off, or rejected. A person who has been abandoned can feel lonely, forgotten, forlorn, or sometimes hopeless.

God, however, says, "I will live among the [people] and won't abandon my people" (1 Kings 6:13). Jesus had a Father who loved Him and didn't abandon Him to permanent death. We have the same Father who gives the same love and care to us He gave to His son Jesus (John 17:23, 26). We have hope in a love that is unfailing (Ps. 147:11). He shows us His love with the forgiveness He offers us. His compassions are new every morning (Lam. 3:22-23). He is merciful and faithful to us (Heb. 2:17). God is a parent who is there for His children. He listens to us attentively: " . . . You will call upon me and come and pray to me and I will listen to you. You will seek me and find me when you seek me with all your heart" (Jer. 29:12-13).

If you are feeling lonely or forgotten this Christmas, call on your heavenly Father. Pray and let Him know how you are and what you need. He will be there for you.

GROUP QUESTIONS: CHAPTER THREE

1. Do you believe God protects you? What ways might He be protecting you that you aren't aware of?

2. Has there been a Christmas when someone hasn't been available to share the holiday with you? What did you do to get through the time?

3. Do you think God hears you when you pray to Him? In what ways has He responded to your prayers before?

4. How would you like your Heavenly Father to take notice of you this Christmas?

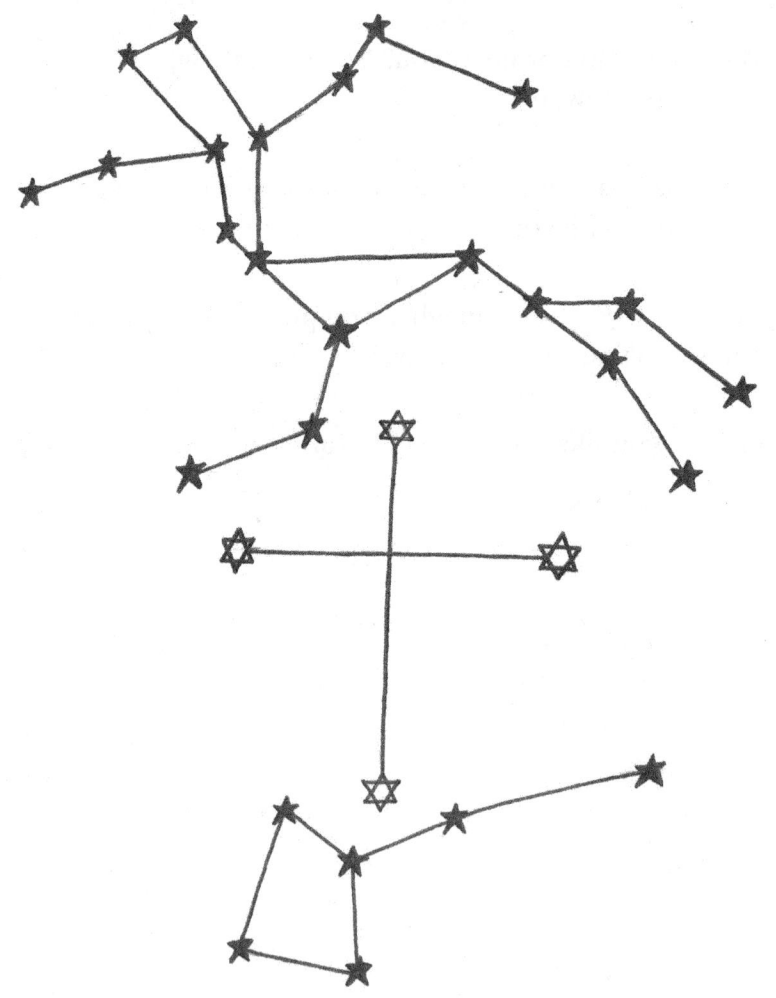

4.

THE CREATOR OF LIFE

"The virgin will be with child and will give birth to a son and they will call him Immanuel, God with us" (Matt. 1:23).

THERE ARE SOME PLACES IN the Biblical story of Jesus where people hesitate and doubt. One of the places is where we read of a virgin birth. What one usually hears with this is the question of how a woman could be pregnant while a virgin? Many will say they don't believe it really happened and will find some other explanation for the account being in the Bible.

Let us consider Luke. There are two women in Luke who have unexpected, miraculous pregnancies. One is Elizabeth, who was barren and well along in years. Her husband, Zechariah, also was an old man. Zechariah and Elizabeth were the parents of John, who came before Jesus. The other woman in Luke is Mary, who was "pledged to be married to a man named Joseph" (Luke 1:27). Note that Mary's question about her pregnancy to the angel who revealed the news was the same as the one other people ask: "How can this be . . . since I am a virgin?" (Luke 1:34).

The angel's answer to this question is "what is conceived in her is from the Holy Spirit" (Matt. 1:20).[5] The genealogy of Jesus Christ in Matthew 1 lists most of the men as fathers. Only one, Joseph, is listed as a husband rather than as a father. The genealogy in Matthew was written to communicate the idea that Jesus was conceived differently from all others.

For those who doubt the birth of a child from a virgin, the answer about the Holy Spirit might be less than satisfactory. The Holy Spirit is often a vague, poorly comprehended idea. What could a spirit do that results in a child? The next part to the answer might be more helpful, as seen in Luke: "Even Elizabeth is going to have a child in her old age. For nothing is impossible with God" (Luke 1:36-37). A child born to a virgin is a miracle and done by God alone. Because He is God, He can do anything.

God would like us to know about who He is. All things were created by Him: "things in heaven and on earth, visible and invisible . . . all things were created by him and for him" (Col. 1:16). He is the Creator, "the Maker of the Bear, and Orion, the Pleiades and the constellations" (Job 9:9). The birth of Jesus to a virgin was also planned and brought about by Him (Isa. 7:14; Matt. 1:23). All of what happened with the birth of Jesus can be because of who God is. We understand this when we understand that He is Creator.

As Creator, the Lord is the originator of life and of time. He started time and will end it. His first coming was prophesied, fulfilled, and is now celebrated at Christmas. The years of our calendar, B.C. and A.D., are dated from His birth. His second coming, which will be the end of our calendar, has also been prophesied.

When He comes the second time, He will decide who enters the kingdom to be with Him and who doesn't. In Hebrews, it says, "Just as man is destined to die once and after that to face judgment, so Christ was sacrificed once to take away the sins of many people; and he will appear a second time, not to bear sin, but to bring salvation to those who are waiting for Him" (Heb. 9:27-28). We can be sure that as His first coming happened the way it was predicted in Scripture, His second coming will be, too: ". . . There will be no more delay! In the days when the seventh angel is about to sound his trumpet, the mystery of God will be accomplished, just as he announced to his servants the prophets" (Rev. 10:6-7).

When God created people, He created the world with a sun, moon, and stars. He also began preparing the glory and splendor of heaven where people could live with Him. This will change when He returns at the end of time, and as it says in Isaiah: "The sun will no more be your light by day, nor will the brightness of the moon shine on you, for the LORD will be your everlasting light . . ." (Isa. 60:19). Those who don't know God and don't obey Him will be "shut out from the presence of the Lord and from the majesty of his power" (2 Thess. 1:9). But those who do know Him will go to live in heaven, a glorious place with His light.

2 Peter 3:5, 7, 10-11 says,

> " . . . by God's word the heavens existed and the earth was formed out of water and by water . . . By the same word the present heavens and earth are reserved for fire, being kept for the day of judgment and destruction of ungodly men . . . But the day of the Lord will come like a thief. The heavens will disappear with a roar; the elements will be destroyed by fire and the earth and everything in it will be laid bare. Since everything will be destroyed in this way, what kind of people ought you to be?"

The passage asks a good question. What are we to do? It goes on to give a good answer: "You ought to live holy and godly lives as you look forward to the day of God . . . since you are looking forward to this, make every effort to be found spotless, blameless and at peace with him" (2 Peter 3:11-12,14). Matthew 24:42, 44 also helps us: "Therefore, keep watch, because you do not know on what day your Lord will come. You also must be ready, because the Son of Man will come at an hour when you do not expect him."

While you are preparing for Christmas, think about whether you are ready for Him, not only with His first coming, but also for His second. God has been preparing the kingdom for us, but we also are to be preparing ourselves so we are ready for the kingdom.

GROUP QUESTIONS: CHAPTER FOUR

1. What do you think of the virgin birth?

2. Read the original account of creation in Genesis 1:1-2. What does it say about what was on earth before creation? What does it say about the presence of the Holy Spirit in creation? What is similar between this passage and Matthew 1:18-20?

3. A lot of energy goes into preparation for Christmas, the celebration of His first coming. Where do you think this energy should be put in preparation for His second coming?

4. We often think of Christmas as a time of peace. If Christ were to come today, would it be when you are at peace with Him (2 Pet. 3:14)?

5.

Great Joy for All People

"Isaiah says 'The Root of Jesse will spring up, one who will arise to rule over the nations; the Gentiles will hope in him'" (Isa. 11:1,10, Rom. 15:12).

THE HEBREW PEOPLE IN THE Bible knew their identity by who their ancestors were. The first of the Hebrew ancestors was Abraham. The name Abraham in Hebrew is "exalted father."[6] The Jews in the New Testament believed they were special because they were descended from this person. They bragged, "We have Abraham as our father" (Matt. 3:9). They were also given the law through Moses, what we read in the first five books of the Old Testament. The Jews believed that the law allowed them to be "a guide for the blind, a light for those who are in the dark, an instructor of the foolish, a teacher of infants . . . " (Rom. 2:19-20). They saw themselves as separate and unique, the only people with a relationship with God.

There was something special about the Jews in that they were given the law, but they often didn't follow it. They could be hypocrites, teaching good things but doing the opposite. The Gentiles who observed them apparently did not think of them as being as spiritual as the Jews liked to think of themselves. Paul criticizes the Jews when he writes, "God's name is blasphemed among the Gentiles because of you" (Rom. 2:24). Romans 3:9 teaches us that Jews are not better than others: "Jews and Gentiles alike are all under sin."

Romans 15:12 says that Gentiles also have a relationship with God: "The Root of Jesse will spring up, one who will arise to rule over the nations; the

Gentiles will hope in him." Who are the Gentiles? The name refers to anyone who is not a Jew. If the Bible has something in it about Gentiles that you do not understand, try changing the word to "all people." For example, compare Isaiah 11:10: "In that day the Root of Jesse will stand as a banner for the peoples; the nations will rally to him" with Romans 15:12: "The Root of Jesse will spring up, one who will arise to rule over the nations; the Gentiles will hope in him". "Gentiles" in Romans 15:12 is understood as the same as "the nations" in Isaiah 11:10. Both are saying that all people will hope in Jesus.

Mark 16:15-16 further states that the good news is for all creation, and that anyone who believes in Christ and is baptized will be saved. God does not just care for people who are directly descended from Abraham, He cares for all people. Jesus came into the world for all of us. Galatians 3:14 says that "He redeemed us in order that the blessing given to Abraham might come to the Gentiles through Jesus Christ." It is great news that Jesus is for all people because all have sinned (Rom. 3:22-23). This is the message of Christmas we find in Luke 2:10-11: " . . . I bring you good news of great joy that will be for <u>all people</u>. Today in the town of David a Savior has been born to you; he is Christ the Lord."

The Jews in Scripture also did not have a correct understanding of how a person comes close to God. They taught that salvation came from following the law, or the rules of what one does outwardly. However, the Bible says that Abraham "believed God and it was credited to him as righteousness" (Rom. 4:3). From the Old Testament through the New, we are taught that, "those who have faith are blessed along with Abraham, the man of faith" (Gal. 3:9).

Usually, a person becomes an heir in a family line if they are born into it. However, as noted above, we do not need to be directly descended from Abraham to be in a relationship with God. All people become a spiritual heir to the promises made to Abraham the same way, by having the kind of faith he had.

The posture of our heart determines what our relationship with God is like. We cannot have communion with God as a result of only external appearances such as going to church or doing good deeds for the poor. Isaiah 29:13 talks about people who "come near to me with their mouth and honor me with their lips, but their hearts are far from me. Their worship is made up of only rules taught by men." In contrast, God looks at what is inside a person. What He would like to know is, where is your heart? Do you really love Him?

The Hebrew people had a Biblical tradition of circumcising their infant boys on the eighth day of life. There is a corresponding idea of spiritual circumcision in Scripture: "The LORD your God will circumcise your hearts and the hearts of your descendants, so that you may love him with all your heart and with all your soul and live" (Deut. 30:6). *The Message*, the Bible in contemporary language, puts it this way: "It's the mark of God in your heart, not of a knife on your skin" that makes a difference. In *The Message* translation, Romans 2:29 says, "A man is a Jew if he is one inwardly; and circumcision is circumcision of the heart, by the Spirit, not by the written code."

We *are* encouraged to study and follow the law of the Lord. Paul, the writer of many of the New Testament books and letters, tried to do this. He writes to the Galatians that he was "advancing in Judaism beyond many Jews of [his] age and was extremely zealous for the traditions of [his] fathers" before his conversion (Gal. 1:14). But when he met Jesus, he learned that if he were going to please God by following rules, he would need to do everything written in the law. Being imperfect, he knew that couldn't be done. He later wrote that the law was there to lead him (and us) to our need for Christ (Gal. 3:24).

Paul summarizes this in Galatians 2:21: " . . . if righteousness could be gained through the law, Christ died for nothing!" If we could be good enough for God by our outward religious practices, there would be no need for a Savior. There would be no need for Jesus to come to earth. There would be no Christmas. But we do have a need for Christmas because we have a need for Christ, His death, and His resurrection.

What religious traditions do you observe? You might be thinking about them more or doing them more because it's Christmas. Are the traditions you practice just lived outwardly or do they come from a faith within? God is interested in what is inside, in your heart, and in whom you hope.

GROUP QUESTIONS: CHAPTER FIVE

1. There are some people who say they have no need for Jesus. What examples of this have you seen? How would you respond to such a person?

2. What religious traditions do you follow at Christmastime that are an expression of your faith, or an outward living out of what is inside? Is there a new one you would like to start? What about it would be fruitful for you right now?

6.

A Spirit of Grace and Supplication

"Seek the LORD while he may be found; call on him while he is near. Let the wicked forsake his way and the evil man his thoughts. Let him turn to the LORD and he will have mercy on him and to our God, for he will freely pardon" (Isa. 55:6-7).

THE LAST CHAPTER TALKED ABOUT where one's heart is. All have sinned and rejected God in some way. Who we love, prize, and delight in or what things we cherish, adore and treasure often are different from what God would like for us. Like it says in Jeremiah 8:6, "Each pursues his own course like a horse charging into battle."

An example of this in the Bible occurred with the Hebrew people. They often had times when they needed help. They would cry out to God and He would send them a leader, such as Moses or Samuel, who served them for a time, but later, they would follow someone different. One example is in 1 Samuel 12 when another country was moving against Israel and they asked the Lord for a king to rule over them. Rejecting God as their king was an "evil thing in the eyes of the Lord" (1 Sam. 12:17). Israel forsook the Lord, spurned the Holy One of Israel and turned their backs on Him. Rather than being left by God, His people left Him. They quit, deserted God, and cast Him off.

Repentance, for Israel, would have been to "return and seek the Lord their God and David their king." They were to come trembling to the Lord and to his blessings (Hosea 3:5). The Lord would like this from us, also, and He sometimes works in remarkable ways to bring people trembling to Him in repentance.

I know a man who went to church for years and by his own testimony was good at doing what others expected from him. He knew what the outward appearance of a churchgoer was and lived that. One spring, his church performed an Easter play about Jesus' death and resurrection. The man was given the role of Caiaphas, the high priest who, along with the teachers of the law, wanted to arrest Jesus and kill Him. On the opening night of the play, this man was backstage waiting for the first lines to start when he had a supernatural experience. He says he knew God was there and it was like he was spiritually stripped bare before Him. He began weeping as the Holy Spirit helped him understand his sin and the grace and forgiveness offered to him by Jesus. A friend was there who prayed with him while he turned his life over to Christ.

The Bible says of these kinds of experiences that when one offers him or herself to God it is "as those who have been brought from death to life" (Rom. 6:13). A fountain is opened to cleanse them from sin and impurity and "God does all these things to a man to turn his soul from the grave, that the light of life may shine on him" (Zech 13:1; Job 33:29-30). When we earnestly come to him asking for forgiveness, He has mercy and freely pardons us (Isa. 55:7). We gain peace and reconciliation with Him (Rom. 5:1,10).

I know another woman who has been a devoted follower of Jesus. She is now retired but worked full-time in a Christian ministry. One year, some friends gave her and her husband money for a vacation in Israel. They greatly enjoyed the trip, visiting many locations where Jesus walked in His life on earth. This woman reports that when she was in the Garden of Gethsemane, where Jesus prayed just before His crucifixion, she heard Him say to her, "I did this for you." She had an immediate feeling of sorrow and found herself saying to Him over and over, "I'm sorry . . . I'm sorry." She too was repenting.

She had no new need for God; she had known Him for many years. But there was still, for her, a spirit of grace and supplication poured out. The Bible says, "They will look on me, the one they have pierced and they will mourn for him . . . and grieve bitterly as one grieves for a firstborn son" (Zech. 12:10). People grieve the crucifixion of Christ when they understand that He died because of them and for their benefit.

There are others in Scripture who have had this kind of experience. Simon Peter, who worked hard all-night fishing and had not caught anything, saw his nets become so full of fish with Jesus' help that the nets began to break. His response was to fall at Jesus' knees: "Go away from me Lord; I am a sinful man!" (Luke 5:4-10). Another man came to Jesus who was covered with leprosy. When he saw Jesus, he fell with his face to the ground and begged Him, "Lord, if you are willing, you can make me clean. Jesus reached out to him. 'I am willing', he said. 'Be clean!' And immediately the leprosy left him" (Luke 5:12-13).

What is in common with these accounts is the spirit of grace and supplication (Zech. 12:10). Supplication is when a person humbly comes to the Lord asking for forgiveness or help. The spirit of grace is what He gives us in return: an assurance that He has forgiven us and restored us to a relationship with Himself.[7]

Some people probably don't think about God through the year. But December, with manger scenes, Christmas carols and the rest, gives us reason to think about Him. Are you a person who is ready for more than thinking just about His existence? Possibly you are ready to repent, forsake your sinful way and come to His. If you are, you might say to Him what is in Psalm 51:

> "Have mercy on me, O God, according to your unfailing love; according to your great compassion blot out my transgression. Wash away all my iniquity and cleanse me from my sin. For I know my transgressions and my sin is always before you. Against you, you only have I sinned and done what is evil in your sight . . . Cleanse me . . . and I will be clean, wash me and I will be whiter than snow

. . . Hide your face from my sins and blot out all my iniquity" (Ps. 51:1-4, 7, 9).

This is the spirit of supplication. When you come to God this way, He sees your broken and contrite heart. He gives you a new, pure heart and a willing spirit. He freely pardons and gives you the joy of salvation. He knows you have come to Him trembling.

GROUP QUESTIONS: CHAPTER SIX

1. Do you know people who have experienced God supernaturally and have been drawn to Him because of the experience? If you do, please share what you can with the group.

2. Read Isaiah 66:2. What times in your life have you gone to Him trembling? How did He answer you?

3. What is your understanding of God's grace? Where have you seen or experienced it?

7.

SELF-SEEKING OR GOD-SEEKING?

> "Come to me, all you who are weary and burdened and I will give you rest. Take my yoke upon you and learn from me, for I am gentle and humble in heart, and you will find rest for your souls. For my yoke is easy and my burden is light" (Matt. 11:28-30).

I HAVE SOME FRIENDS WHO work on a university campus with international students. The students come to the United States for an education that will give them better job prospects when they return home. Some come from countries where they are not allowed to ask questions about the government or other religions like Christianity. While they are in the States, there is opportunity for them to learn more.

For example, on a recent election day, some of the international students stood near a polling place, watching with great interest how leaders are democratically chosen in the U.S. As a second example, those who drive international students to and from the airport report that when they arrive, the students often ask for a Bible in the short time it takes them to get to campus, before they even get to their new home. The Bible is a book they can't get in their country. The students come looking for it and new ways of doing things. They are seekers.

People of all nationalities seek things, from possessions to information and ideas to relationships. The Bible asks us a question about this: what are you trying to find? What is your heart and mind set on (Col. 3:1-2)? Are you seeking self or seeking God?

Self-seekers are lovers of themselves and pleasure rather than lovers of God and what He says is good. They love money and may be boastful, proud, or conceited about who they are or what they have (2 Tim. 3:1-5). Mark 4:19 says that " . . . the worries of this life, the deceitfulness of wealth and the desires for other things come in and choke the word, making it unfruitful in their lives." For some, this happens more at Christmas. At the time one would think people would be thinking more about God, it can be where there is no room for God (Ps. 10:4).

In contrast, God-seekers put their hope in God. They have heard Jesus say, "Do not worry, saying 'What shall we eat?' or 'What shall we drink?' or "What shall we wear? For [others] run after all these things and your heavenly Father knows you need them. But seek first his kingdom and his righteousness, and all these things will be given you as well" (Matt. 6:31-33).

People who spend time and energy on possessions and pleasure become weary and burdened. They can wear themselves out running after these things. This is what many of us experience at Christmas. Rather than being a time to enjoy, Christmas is a time to become exhausted when shopping. What God says to those who are weary of this and other things is, "Come to me . . . and I will give you rest . . . learn from me . . . my yoke is easy and my burden is light" (Matt. 11:28-30).

This Christmas, think about what your heart and mind are set on. Are you ready to seek Him rather than self? What would it be like for you to make room for Him and seek His kingdom first? When you do so, you will find rest.

GROUP QUESTIONS: CHAPTER SEVEN

1. Do you usually draw closer to God or are you farther away from Him in the Christmas season? What have you found that helps with this?

2. What things are your heart and mind often set on that are in the way of your relationship with God? That is, what are the worries of this life or desires for other things that might choke the Word for you?

3. In what ways do you seek first His kingdom at Christmas?

4. What else have you found that helps you experience God's rest in the Christmas season?

8.

The Foundation Stone

" . . . They stumbled over the 'stumbling stone'. As it is written, 'See, I lay in Zion a stone that causes men to stumble and a rock that makes them fall and the one who trusts in him will never be put to shame'" (Rom. 9:32-33).

THE JEWS IN THE BIBLE were waiting for the Messiah, a king who would deliver them and be the redemption of Israel. Some believed that Jesus was the Messiah; many did not. Some Jewish people are still waiting and looking for someone other than Jesus.

Why did they reject the idea that Jesus was the Messiah prophesied in the Old Testament? Paul says in Romans 10:2-3 that " . . . I can testify about them that they are zealous for God, but their zeal is not based on knowledge. Since they did not know the righteousness that comes from God and sought to establish their own, they did not submit to God's righteousness." As discussed earlier, Jews in the Bible worked at keeping the law. They believed that that was how they would be acceptable to God. But Romans 10:4 says that a works-based faith doesn't work because "Christ is the end of the law so that there may be righteousness for everyone who believes." Being right with God occurs only when a person believes in Jesus and confesses that He is Lord. Righteousness comes by faith, by trusting that He has forgiven you of sin. The Jews did not understand the idea that righteousness come from God alone and not by their good deeds, and along with it, missed who Jesus was and why He came.

In numerous places in the Bible, Jesus is referred to as a stone or rock. For those who missed who Jesus was, He was a stumbled-over stone. For those in generations past or present who believe in Him, He is instead a foundation stone and a Rock to trust (Isa. 8:14; 2 Sam. 23:3; Ps. 118:22; Matt. 21:42; Rom. 9:32-33; 1 Pet. 2:6).

The Temple in the Old Testament had an actual foundation stone under the room called the Holy of Holies, the innermost location of God's presence and mercy seat. In the New Testament, we who have the Spirit living in us are God's temple and Jesus is the foundation of our faith (1 Cor. 3:11, 16-17). Jesus is the Living Stone, "rejected by men but chosen by God and precious to him" (1 Pet. 2:4).

He is the dear, beloved one of inestimable value: "See, I lay in Zion a chosen and precious cornerstone" (Isa. 28:16). What is precious about Him is the life he gave. First Peter 1:18-19 says, "You know that it was not with perishable things such as silver or gold that you were redeemed from the empty way of life . . . but with the precious blood of Christ, a lamb without blemish or defect."

Sacred stones in Scripture are used to build altars, sometimes to other gods or idols (Deut. 16:22; 1 Kings 14:23; Hosea 10:1-2). In the 2000s, we do not have sacred stones the same way as those in the Bible, but we still have foundation stones in the houses we live in. Great houses and fine mansions have stones bought with a large amount of money and energy. Since they require much from us, these house foundations may be close to being sacred stones. Even if they are, great houses and fine mansions are common. There are many of them in the U.S. and if a person decided to sell one, there are others one could buy.

This is different from God and the house He has prepared for us. The house God gives us also has many rooms but it is holy and unique (John 14:2-3). And "there is [only] one God and one mediator between God and men, the man Christ Jesus, who gave himself as a ransom for all men" so they can be in

God's house (1 Tim. 2:5). Jesus, the foundation stone, is a unique sacred stone. There isn't anything that is valuable to us the way Jesus is valuable to us.

At Christmas, we think about giving gifts and can spend large amounts of time looking for what to give those to whom we are close. We would like to find gifts that please our family and friends. Moms and dads show love for their children by finding what has been requested, looking for what is just right for their child.

God does this also, but even more than we do: "Which of you fathers, if your son asks for a fish, will give him a snake instead? Or if he asks for an egg, will give him a scorpion? If you then, though you are evil, know how to give good gifts to your children, how much more will your Father in heaven give the Holy Spirit to those who ask him!" (Luke 11:11-13). He gives to us when we ask: "Ask and it will be given to you; seek and you will find; knock and the door will be opened to you. For everyone who asks receives, he who seeks finds and to him who knocks, the door will be opened" (Luke 11:9-10).

We are rich when we know God. The poorest of the poor have sin forgiven and receive an inheritance of riches and wealth greater than gold (Isa. 14:30; 1 Pet. 1:4-7). In Jesus, He has not given us a stumbling stone but rather, the precious and unique gift of life.

GROUP QUESTIONS: CHAPTER EIGHT

1. What is precious or valuable to you?

2. What kind of gifts do you like to receive? How do you decide what gifts to give?

3. In what ways is Jesus valuable to you?

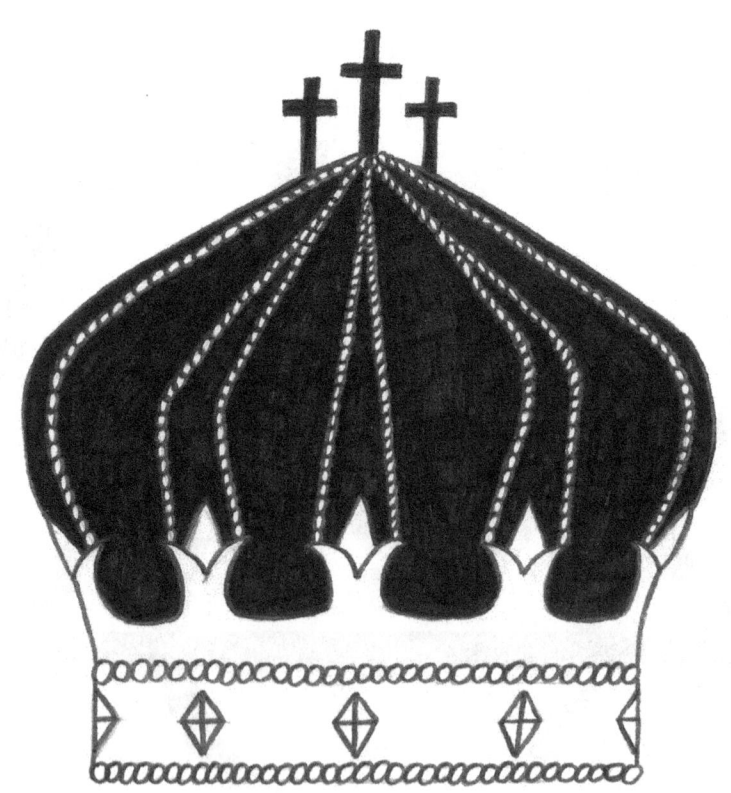

9.

Jesus the Compassionate King

"Their hearts weren't loyal to him; they weren't faithful to his covenant. Yet he was merciful; he forgave their iniquities and did not destroy them" (Ps. 78:37-38).

THERE IS MORE HISTORY TO the Jews' rejection of Jesus as Messiah. God chose His people but they had difficulty following Him. They were forgetful of the wonders He had shown them, rebellious and sinful, disbelieving and distrustful, and disloyal and faithless. God was their king but they asked for another. They anointed Saul as their first human king, but the Lord later rejected Saul because he rejected the word of the Lord (1 Sam. 15:26). So God chose David, the son of Jesse of Bethlehem (1 Sam. 16:1-13). After David, there were other kings—some were good but three-fourths of them were evil.

Finally, God "gave his people over to the sword" (Ps. 78:62). The nation was sent out of the land into exile in a foreign country because of their sin (2 Kings 24:3-4). With the exile, it was decided that "the nation which had produced mighty rulers in the past now would have no king. After Zedekiah was overthrown by Babylon, no king from the Davidic dynasty replaced him."[8] Thus, there was not a king from the line of Judah from 586 B.C. until Jesus centuries later (2 Kings 24:17; Jer. 52:1-11).

But God did not leave His people without a king in exile in Babylon. He had compassion on them. Once again, He settled them in their own land. He brought them back "into the bond of the covenant" by giving them one more king from the line of David (Ezek. 20:37). The last to come out of the Hebrew nation was a strong branch "fit for a ruler's scepter," Jesus, a better, permanent king (Ezek. 19:11). Psalm 78:68, 70, 72 says, "He chose the tribe of Judah . . . He chose David his servant to be the shepherd of his people. And David shepherded them . . . with skillful hands he led them."⁹

Isaiah 14:25 prophecies that the yoke or burden of a foreign ruler will end: "I will crush the Assyrian . . . His yoke will be taken from my people and his burden removed from their shoulders." Jesus spoke similar words: "Come to me, all you who are weary and burdened, and I will give you rest. Take my yoke upon you and learn from me, for I am gentle and humble in heart, and you will find rest for your souls. For my yoke is easy and my burden is light" (Matt. 11:28-30). Notice what a person learns by reading these passages together. Jesus used these words to say there's no need to wait or look for another king. He was who was prophesied in Isaiah 14. He came to shatter the yoke that burdens us and give rest to our souls.

You might think that you have not been in revolt against God like the Israelites in the Old Testament. Still, there is possibly another difficulty in your relationship with God: complacency. Sometimes we feel secure and don't notice what we should about our sin. Christmas is a time when it is easy to be complacent. All around us are decorations, music, and stories that are in some way about the baby Jesus. But at the same time, we can be like those in Amos 6:4-6 who "lie on beds inlaid with ivory and lounge on couches. You dine on choice lambs and fattened calves. You strum away on harps like David and improvise on musical instruments. You drink wine by the bowlful and use the finest lotions, but don't grieve over . . . ruin."

What if we do not see our sin? God still sees it: "I know how many are your offenses and how great are your sins" (Amos 5:12). He gave Israel kings from the line of David but when they did not see their sin, He sent them out of their land into exile without a king. Note that the complacent and secure are among the first to go into exile (Amos 6:7).

For those who do see their need and come to Jesus, He is a compassionate king who forgives sin. Like with those in the Old Testament, Jesus does not destroy us when we sin. He made atonement by giving His life for all we have done. He is a merciful king who has put the government on His shoulders rather than the yoke across ours (Isa. 9:2-7).

There is a difference between serving Him and serving kings of other lands (2 Chron. 12:8). Other kings break promises and agreements; they go to war with those who should be their brothers (e.g. Rehoboam in 2 Chron. 11:4). They can be unfaithful and reject what is right. It says in Hosea 10:7 that "Samaria and its king will float away like a twig on the surface of the waters;" all earthly kingdoms are temporary.

Jesus the everlasting king is compassionate, loving and gracious (Lam. 3:22-23; Neh. 9:17). He calls us His brothers (Heb. 2:11). Righteousness is the scepter of His kingdom (Heb. 1:8). He came to serve and listens to us attentively (Mark 10:45; Jer. 29:12-3). He saves, comforts, and gives hope (1 Sam. 17:47; Dan. 3:29; 2 Cor. 1:3, 10). He works with us so that we do not lose heart but are renewed inwardly day by day (2 Cor. 4:16). Can you think of another king you would rather come to than one with the compassion Jesus has for us?

GROUP QUESTIONS: CHAPTER NINE

1. To be complacent is to be pleased or satisfied with oneself, possibly even smug. What happens to us if we are this way with God?

2. Where are you complacent in your relationship with the Lord? What would you like to change in your lifestyle or mindset that prompts you to move away from complacency and to the Lord?

3. What is a personal example of when a person showed compassion to you?

4. How would it change your understanding of God if you didn't think He was compassionate?

10.

WHO DO YOU SAY I AM?

"Men of Athens, I see that in every way you are very religious. For I even found an altar with this inscription: 'TO AN UNKNOWN GOD'. Now what you worship as something unknown I am going to proclaim to you" (Acts 17:22-23).

ONE FALL, I WAS AT an art show where there was an artist who worked with metals. He had made the metal into small statues that looked like people in an ancient Egyptian drawing. He was selling them as gods and goddesses. The practice of making idols was a common problem in the Old Testament. The Bible asks, "Of what value is an idol, since a man has carved it? For he who makes it trusts in his own creation; he makes idols that cannot speak. Woe to him who says to wood 'Come to life!' Or to lifeless stone, 'Wake up!' Can it give guidance? It is covered with gold and silver; there is no breath in it" (Hab. 2:18-19). I was thinking about this while I was looking at those small metal statues: how could something made out of a piece of metal do anything for a person? It says in the Bible, "The towns of Judah and the people of Jerusalem will go and cry out to the gods to whom they burn incense, but they will not help them at all when disaster strikes" (Jer. 11:12).

Jesus isn't like any of these. Rather than being lifeless, He is the Creator of life. It says in Acts 17:25 that "He himself gives all men life and breath and everything else." Jesus "sustains all things by his powerful word" (Heb. 1:3). He has been "found worthy of greater honor than Moses, just as the builder of a house has greater honor than the house itself" (Heb. 3:3).

Jesus is the better, permanent King from the line of David. He is the royal son, the radiance of God's glory and the exact representation of His being (Ps. 72:1; Heb. 1:3). He has the keys to life in the kingdom (Isa. 22:22; Rev. 3:7) and death or Hades (Job 38:12; Rev. 1:18). He is the beloved prince who tells us what He has seen in the Father's presence (Dan. 7:13; Song of Songs 5:9-16; John 8:40). As in earlier chapters, His reign in the kingdom is one of justice and righteousness. Psalm 72:17 says, " . . . all nations will be blessed through him and they will call him blessed."

Scripture also helps us with questions like whether Jesus was just an ordinary man with special gifts or just a good teacher. We were given prophecies so we can know for sure who Jesus is. In *More Than A Carpenter*, Josh McDowell writes that both Jesus and writers of the New Testament books "appealed to the prophecies of the Old Testament to substantiate his claims as the Messiah."[10] The identity of Jesus was made clear by an angel when He was born: "today in the town of David a Savior has been born to you; he is Christ the Lord" (Luke 2:11). This passage says Jesus is the Savior, and He is the Messiah. The idea that Jesus was just a good teacher is not found in Scripture.

Jesus is supreme, higher and greater than us, but also merciful and faithful as our high priest. We can put our hope in Him. He defends the afflicted and saves the needy and their children: "He will be like rain falling on a mown field, like showers watering the earth" (Ps. 72:4, 6). There isn't a religion or idol that helps like Jesus.

I learned more about this when my son started college. The first months were lonely ones for him. He spent time in his room by himself between classes, struggled with longing to be home, and didn't sleep or eat well. I fasted and prayed for him and soon found that God was answering my prayers.

A friend asked my son to assist him with planning a creative devotion about the persecuted church. My son loves drama and costumes and had an opportunity to lead other students in a role-play about the subject. A few days later God gave him another opportunity to be involved in a conversation about a subject he enjoyed: relationships between Muslims and Christians. The men talking about it stood right outside his door in the hall where he could hear them.

These sweet moments came the same week I was fasting and praying for him and so began the start of his finding friends. The poor of the earth can come to Him as they are, with their need and weaknesses laid before Him. They are those who mourn, who are meek, who hunger or thirst and who are pure in heart (Matt. 5:3-8). My son was all of these and God was, for him, merciful and faithful. He bestowed "a crown of beauty instead of ashes, the oil of gladness instead of mourning and a garment of praise instead of despair" (Isa. 61:3). Scripture says these kinds of events happen so "that we might not rely on ourselves but on God who raises the dead" (2 Cor. 1:9).

Believing in Jesus is different than being religious. This Christmas Jesus can be more for you than an unknown god or a baby in a story. Jesus is someone who is really here with us. "The virgin will be with child and will give birth to a son. They will call him Immanuel—which means 'God with us'" (Matt. 1:23).

In a conversation with His disciples found in Mark 8, Jesus asked them, "Who do people say I am?" They replied, "Some say John the Baptist, others say Elijah and still others, one of the prophets." Jesus then asked them, "But what about you? Who do you say I am?" This question is not just about the religion of other people, it is a question for you.

GROUP QUESTIONS: CHAPTER TEN

1. If you are one who thinks of Jesus as only an ordinary person with special gifts or as a good teacher, what do you do with the announcement of the angel in Luke 2:11? Why would there be a story like this in the Bible that is made up?

2. The question of Jesus' identity is one of the weightiest questions a person will decide on in their lifetime. Read what Christ said about who He was in Luke 22:66-71 and John 4:25-26. If Christ were to meet you where you could see Him today and ask you "Who do you say I am?" what would your answer be?

11.

Doing the Unexpected

"Comfort, comfort my people, says your God. Speak tenderly to Jerusalem, and proclaim to her that her hard service has been completed, that her sin has been paid for . . . He gives strength to the weary and increases the power of the weak . . . Those who hope in the LORD will renew their strength. They will soar on wings like eagles; they will run and not grow weary, they will walk and not be faint" (Isa. 40:1-2; 29-31).

I WROTE THIS DEVOTION ON the eighth anniversary of my late husband's death. When I started it, I knew I had just eight weeks to write it and I had not written a devotion before. When looking at the calendar, it seemed like this would be the year to write a book to honor my husband's life, and I asked God to help me get this done, knowing that just before Christmas, there were other things to do, too.

What was different about writing this was that the work was done without an outline of subjects. For a number of years, I've had a morning quiet time by opening the Bible and reading where it opens. I ask God to show me what He would like me to be thinking about. When I'm done with a section, I turn the pages and read the next section He shows me. The main ideas start coming together and when I turn to a section that doesn't follow from the ones before, I know God is done thinking with me for the time. God has kept the ideas on logical, understandable subjects each morning. For this book, He led me in the same way. My daily reading of Scripture informed these chapters.

Then He did the unexpected: He finished in two weeks. When I got to Isaiah 14:25 and Matthew 11:28-30 about finding rest for your souls (Chapter Nine), the Scriptures about Jesus, which had been coming daily, stopped. He was done and the subject changed to rest. He gave me a yoke that was easy, one I had learned from my reading would come from the prophesied Messiah. He made what might have been hard or heavy to carry lighter (1 Kings 12:1-15).

In the last chapter, we explored the idea that God is both supremely above us and with us. Jesus, He who saves, is also Immanuel, God with us. He is a king who is a servant to His people (John 13:1-16). God gave me a banquet of knowledge about Himself and then proclaimed a holiday. He "distributed gifts with royal liberality," which included the gift of rest (Esther 2:18). This idea changed my thinking about Christmas.

Christmas, for me, now isn't the usual, a time to be busy. It has become a time for understanding what rest is: rest from sin and rest from work; a time for having joy in who Jesus is and what He came to do. Ezekiel 37:28 says, "The nations will know that I the LORD make Israel holy when my sanctuary is among them forever." As a sanctuary, God shelters His people. He watches over us and takes care of us. He is in our midst to help us in the ways we need. This Christmas, may you, too, find Him doing the unexpected in your life in ways that show you He is a sanctuary.

GROUP QUESTIONS: CHAPTER ELEVEN

1. What in your life do you see that says to you that Jesus is Immanuel, God with you?

2. In what ways has the King also been a servant to you?

3. For you, what is it to rest and experience joy for Christmas? How would you go about that?

4. Now that this book is done, what would you like to say to the Lord this Christmas?

Endnotes

1. Most passages of Scripture are from the *Scofield Study Bible*, New International Version (NIV), Oxford University Press, 1984. This edition was before gender language in the NIV was changed. Some Scripture is from *The Message, The Bible in Contemporary Language* by Eugene H. Peterson, NavPress, 2002. Where there is a translation other than the 1984 NIV, there is a note in the text.

2. *The Scofield Study Bible*, New International Version, "How to Use This Study Bible," Oxford University Press, New York, New York, 2004, pp. xi-xii.

3. *Complete Jewish Bible, an English Version of the Old Testament and New Testament.* Translation by David H. Stern, Jewish New Testament Publications, Clarksville, Maryland and Jerusalem, Israel, 1998, pp. xliii-xlvii.

4. "The Christ" (Greek *christos*) and "the Messiah" (Hebrew *masiah*) both mean "the Anointed One." *The Scofield Study Bible*, New International Version, Oxford University Press, N.Y., New York, 2004, p. 1341.

5. Matthew 1:18-24 is a passage parallel to Luke 1:26-38. Luke 1:35 says, "The Holy Spirit will come upon you and the power of the Most High will overshadow you. So the holy one to be born will be called the Son of God." Matthew 1:18-24 has different wording that clarifies what is being said, i.e., the child was conceived by the Holy Spirit.

6. *Interpreter's Dictionary of the Bible*, Volume 1, Abingdon Press, Nashville, Tennessee, 1962, p.15.

7. If you would like to hear about other people who have come to God in the same way, watch the online video "The Cross" by the Billy Graham Evangelistic Association. It shares the stories of two other people who experienced what it was like to see their sin and the mercy of God at the same time.

8. *The Bible Knowledge Commentary,* Old Testament, John F. Walvoord and Roy B. Zuck, editors, Victor Books Publications, 1983, p.1263.

9. David sometimes refers to the king in the Old Testament and sometimes is a foreshadowing of Jesus. Theologians say David is a "type" of Christ. In Psalm 78:70, 72, the name David refers to both king David and Jesus. *The New International Dictionary of New Testament Theology,* Vol. 3, Colin Brown, General Editor, Zondervan Publishing House, Grand Rapids, Michigan, 1978, pp. 903-907.

10. McDowell, Josh. *More Than A Carpenter,* Tyndale House Publishers, Wheaton, Illinois, 1977, p.101.

About the Artwork by Matthew Reierson

A Sanctuary in Our Midst - Title page

The illustration is a two-in-one image of a cathedral/stable with an altar/manger inside.

Ch. 1 - Introduction

" . . . be prepared in season and out of season . . . " (2 Tim. 4:2).

The symbols surrounding the cross, clockwise from upper right, represent spring, summer fall and winter. The image is meant to raise the question: when is Scripture not in season? The arms of the cross are of equal length in all four directions, suggesting the Bible is equally in season all four seasons.

Ch. 2 - Good Tidings: Jesus Has Come

"The desert and parched land will be glad; the wilderness will rejoice and blossom. Like the crocus, it will burst into bloom . . . " (Isaiah 35:1-2).

The three crosses and three fish both represent the Trinity. The image is meant to resemble a crocus flower as it comes up in the spring.

Ch. 3 - A Loved Child

The image is a version of Michelangelo's Creation of Adam from the Sistine Chapel, rotated so the arm of God is reaching down to the arm of man. The arm of man is drawn smaller to make it look more like a child's arm. The stars are a reference to God's promise to Abraham that his descendants (i.e., his children) would be as numerous as the stars with twelve stars to indicate the twelve tribes of Israel (Gen. 15:5).

Ch. 4 - The Creator of Life

"He is the Maker of the Bear, and Orion, the Pleiades and the constellations . . . " (Job 9:9).

The image is of the constellation Crux (the Cross), designated by stars of David. The surrounding constellations give the context of where this constellation is located in the sky.

Ch. 5 - Great Joy for All People

"The Root of Jesse will spring up, one who will arise to rule over the nations; the Gentiles will hope in him" (Rom. 15:12).

The mirror image of a tree with its branches growing up and its roots growing down is meant to resemble a Jewish menorah.

Ch. 6 - A Spirit of Grace and Supplication

"Afterward the Israelites will return and seek the Lord their God and David their king. They will come trembling to the LORD and to his blessings in the last days" (Hosea 3:5).

The image is a U-turn symbol within a heart, representing how repentance is a sinful (i.e. black-hearted) individual making a turnaround in their life.

Ch. 7 - Self-seeking or God-seeking?

"For my yoke is easy and my burden is light" (Matt. 11:30).

The arms of the cross are an ox's yoke.

Ch. 8 - The Foundation Stone

"They stumbled over the stumbling stone" (Rom. 9:32).

The first symbol of the Trinity is made to look like a warning sign for rockslides.

"... a chosen and precious cornerstone" (Is. 28:16).

The second symbol of the Trinity holds a crystalline gemstone whose facets are meant to resemble the Star of David.

Ch. 9 - Jesus the Compassionate King

"You are a forgiving God, gracious and compassionate..." (Neh. 9:17).

The illustration is a two-in-one image of a crown and Calvary, referring to Jesus being crucified because He was "King of the Jews." His crucifixion for the sins of mankind was the ultimate act of compassion.

Ch. 10 – Who Do You Say I Am?

"I even found an altar with this inscription "TO AN UNKNOWN GOD" (Acts 17:22).

The image is of an ancient Greek altar with the Greek words: "Se enan agnōsto theo" ("To an unknown god").

Ch. 11 - Doing the Unexpected

"Comfort, comfort my people,' says your God ... They will soar on wings like eagles ..." (Is. 40:1, 31).

The Hebrew words on the eagle read "Comfort my people."

For more information about
Karen L. Straszheim
and
A Sanctuary in our Midst
please visit:

www.facebook.com/A-Sanctuary-In-Our-Midst-1095584350624207

For more information about
AMBASSADOR INTERNATIONAL
please visit:

www.ambassador-international.com
@AmbassadorIntl
www.facebook.com/AmbassadorIntl

If you enjoyed this book, please consider leaving us a review on Amazon, Goodreads, or our website.

www.ingramcontent.com/pod-product-compliance
Lightning Source LLC
Chambersburg PA
CBHW070758050426
42452CB00012B/2391